THIS COLORING BOOK BELONGS TO:

1
2
3
4
5
6
7
8
9
10
11
12
13
14
15
16
17
18
19
20
21
22

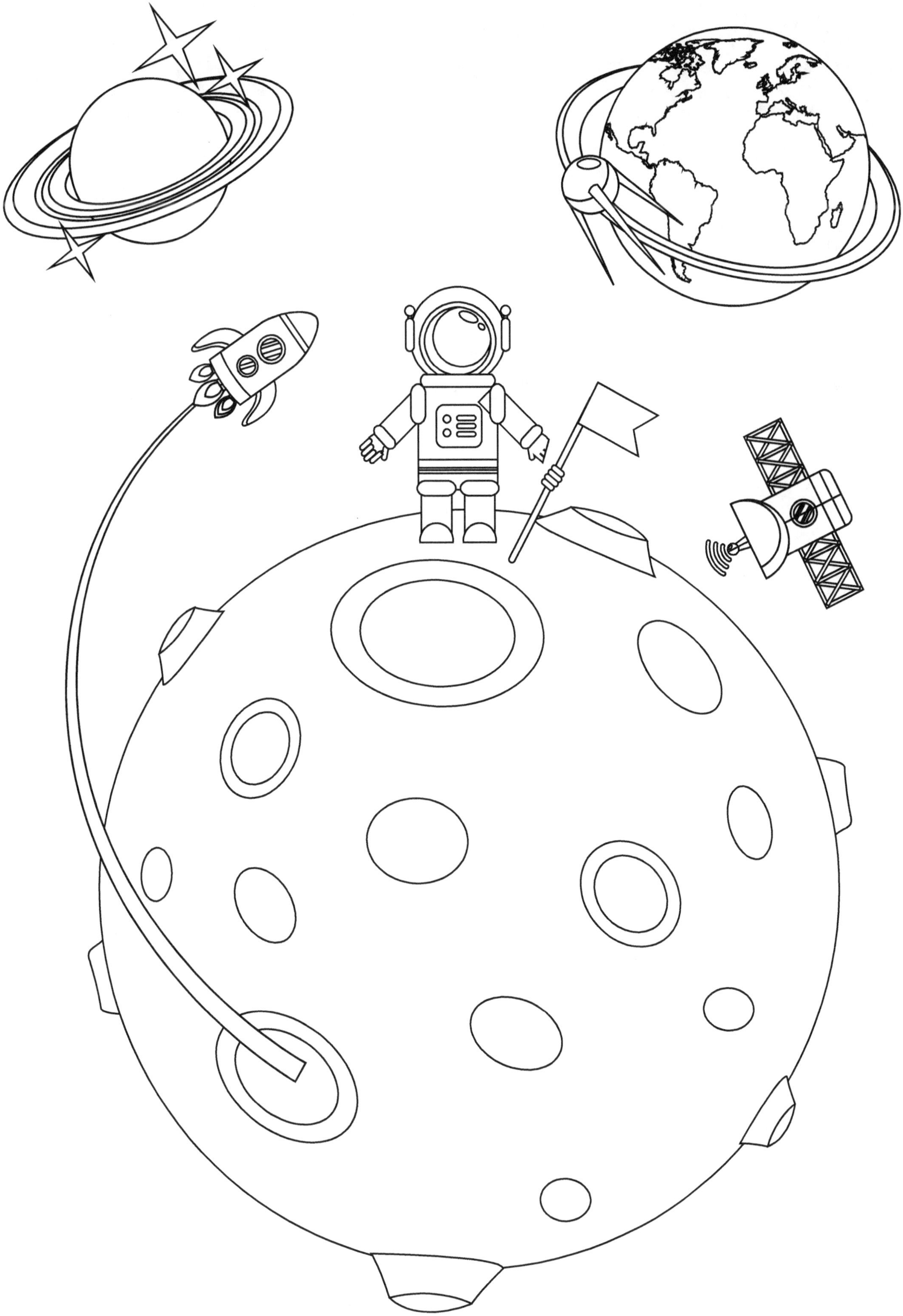

038

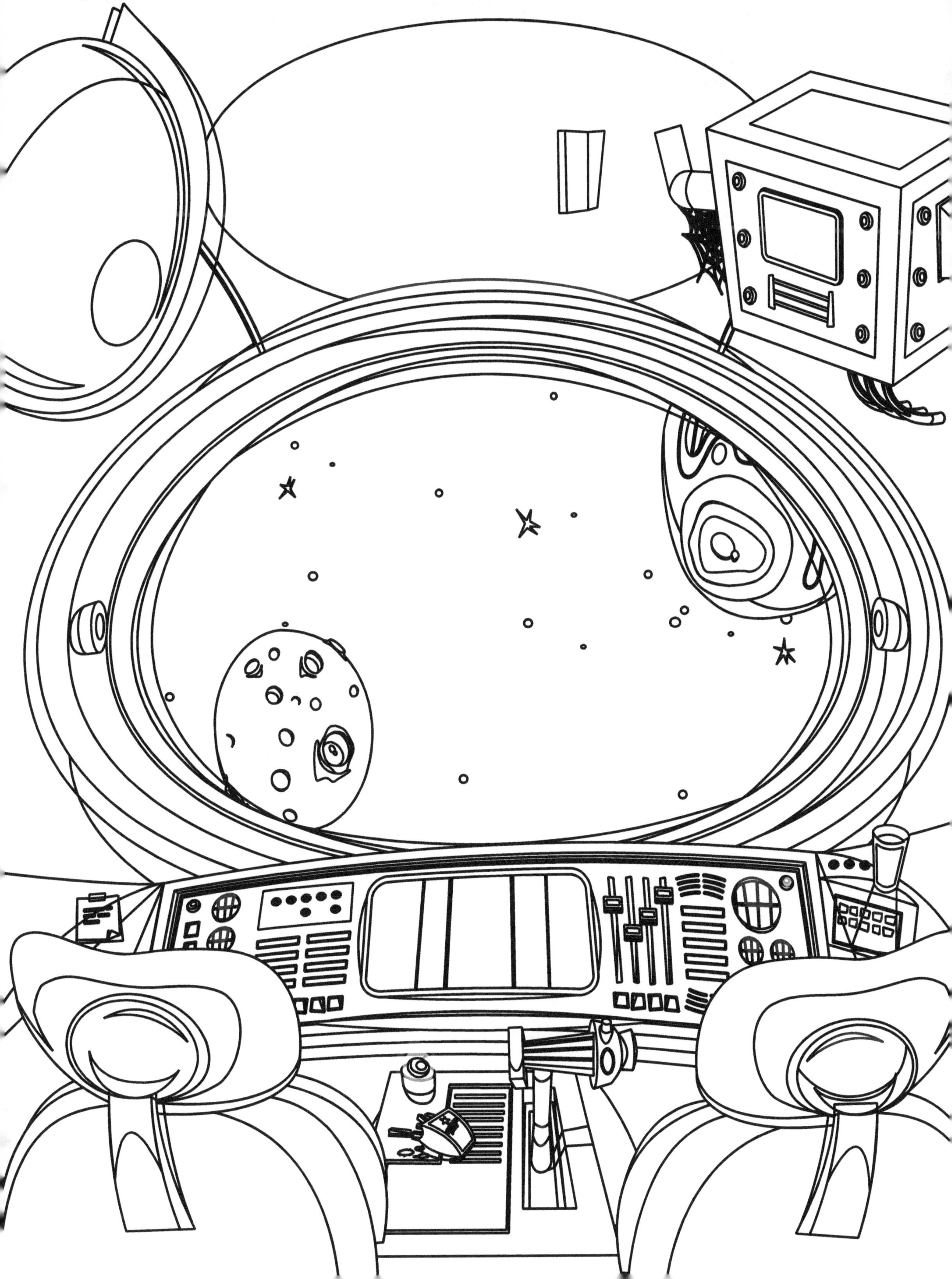

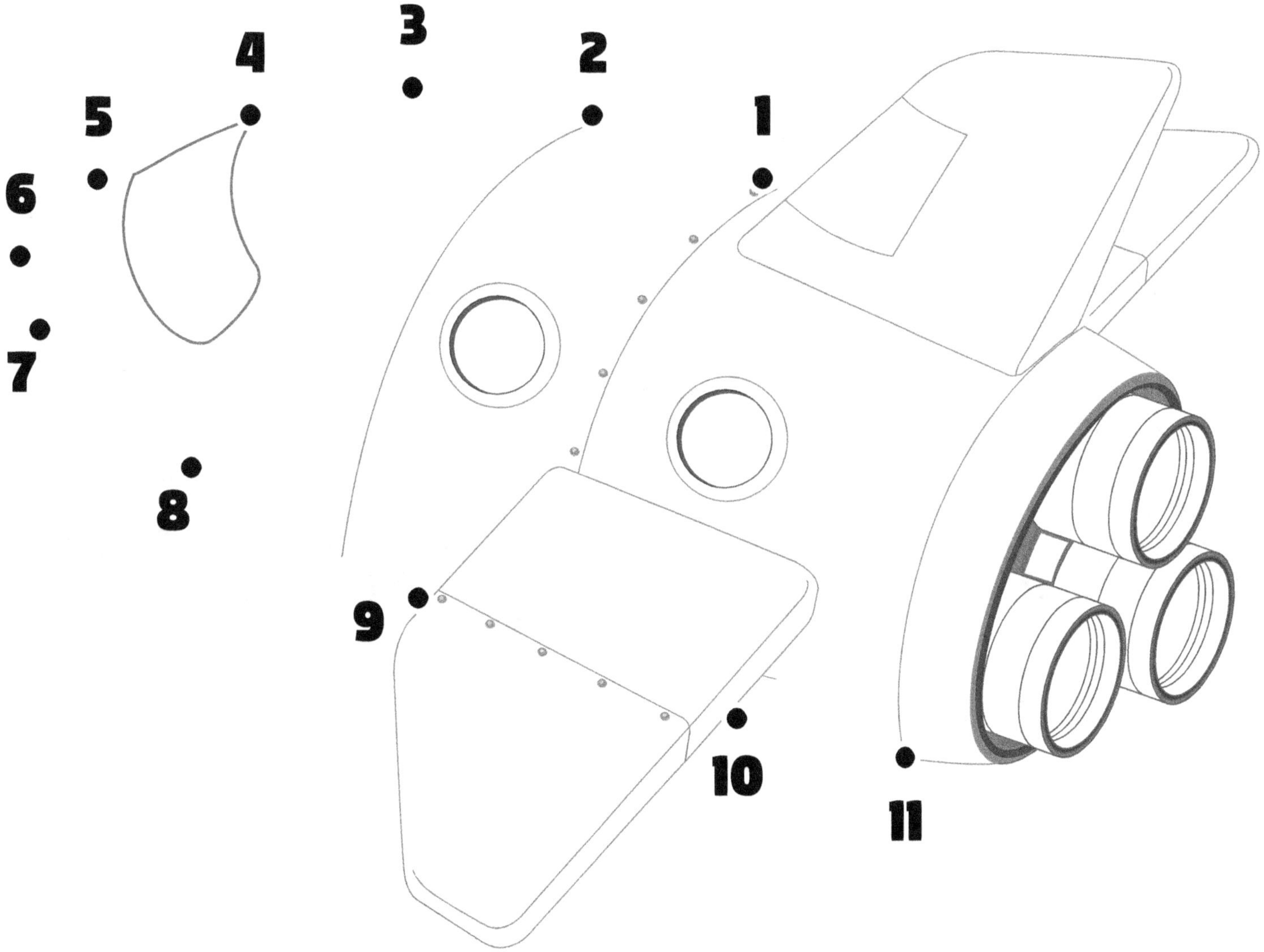
1
2
3
4
5
6
7
8
9
10
11

1
2
3

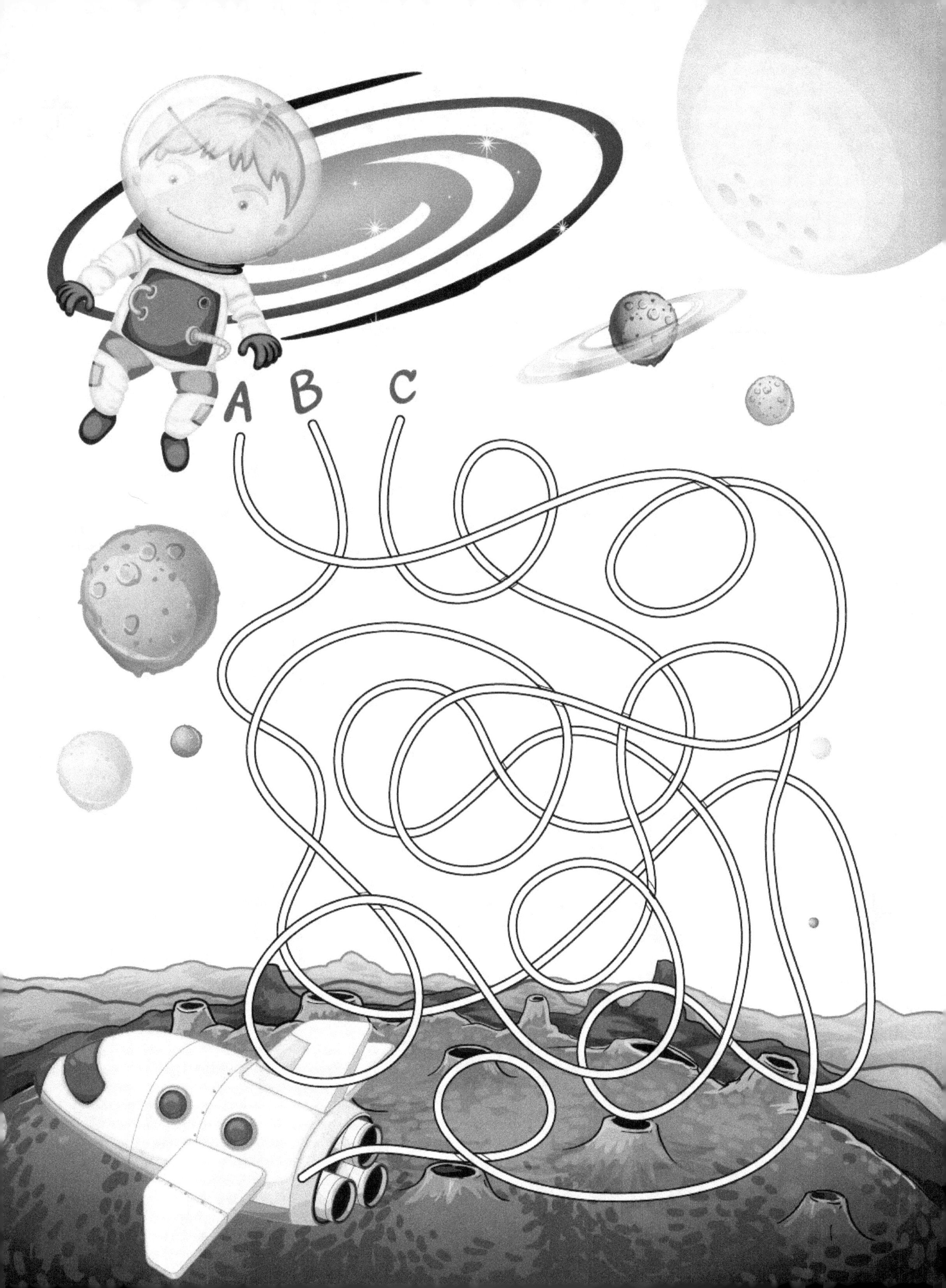
A B C

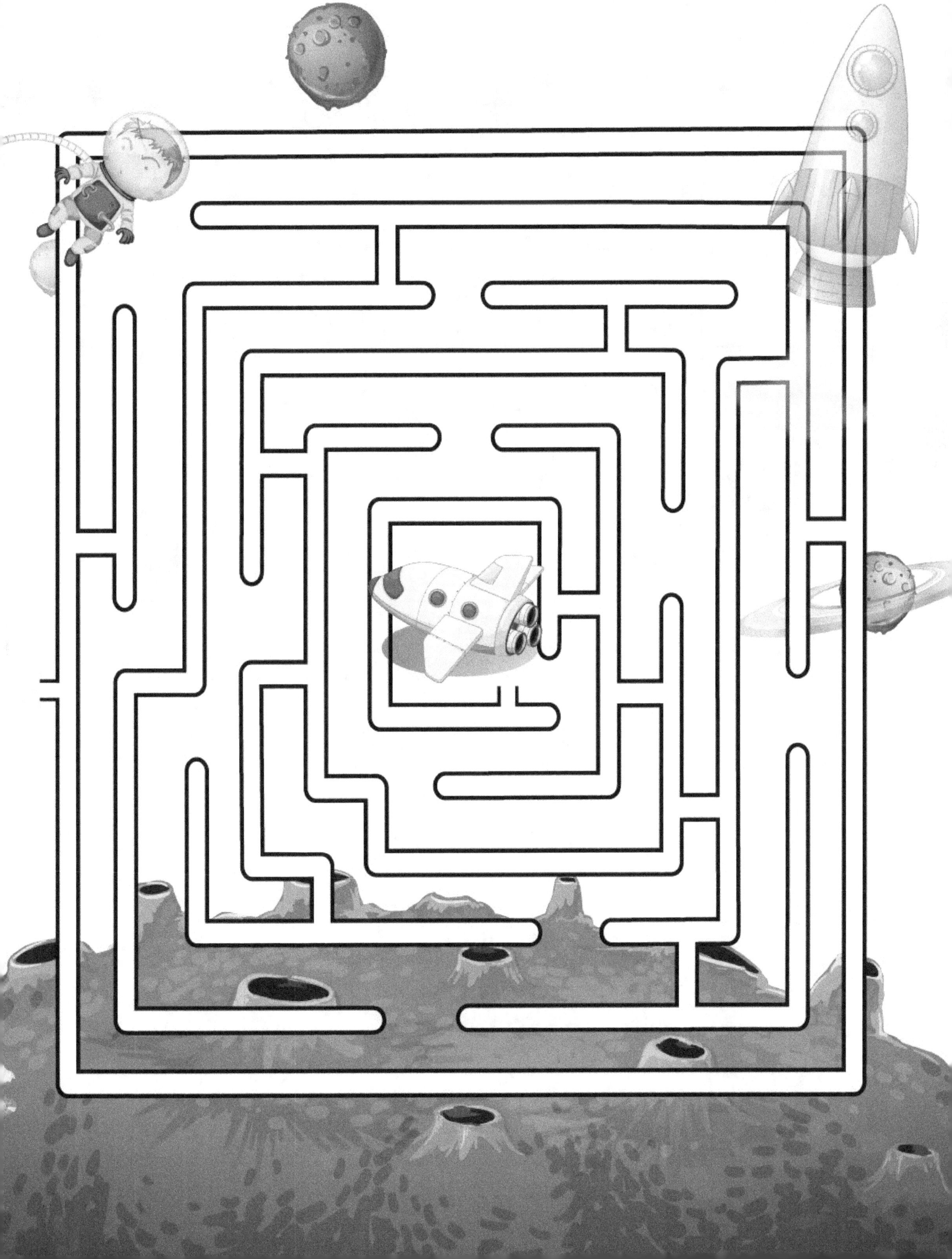

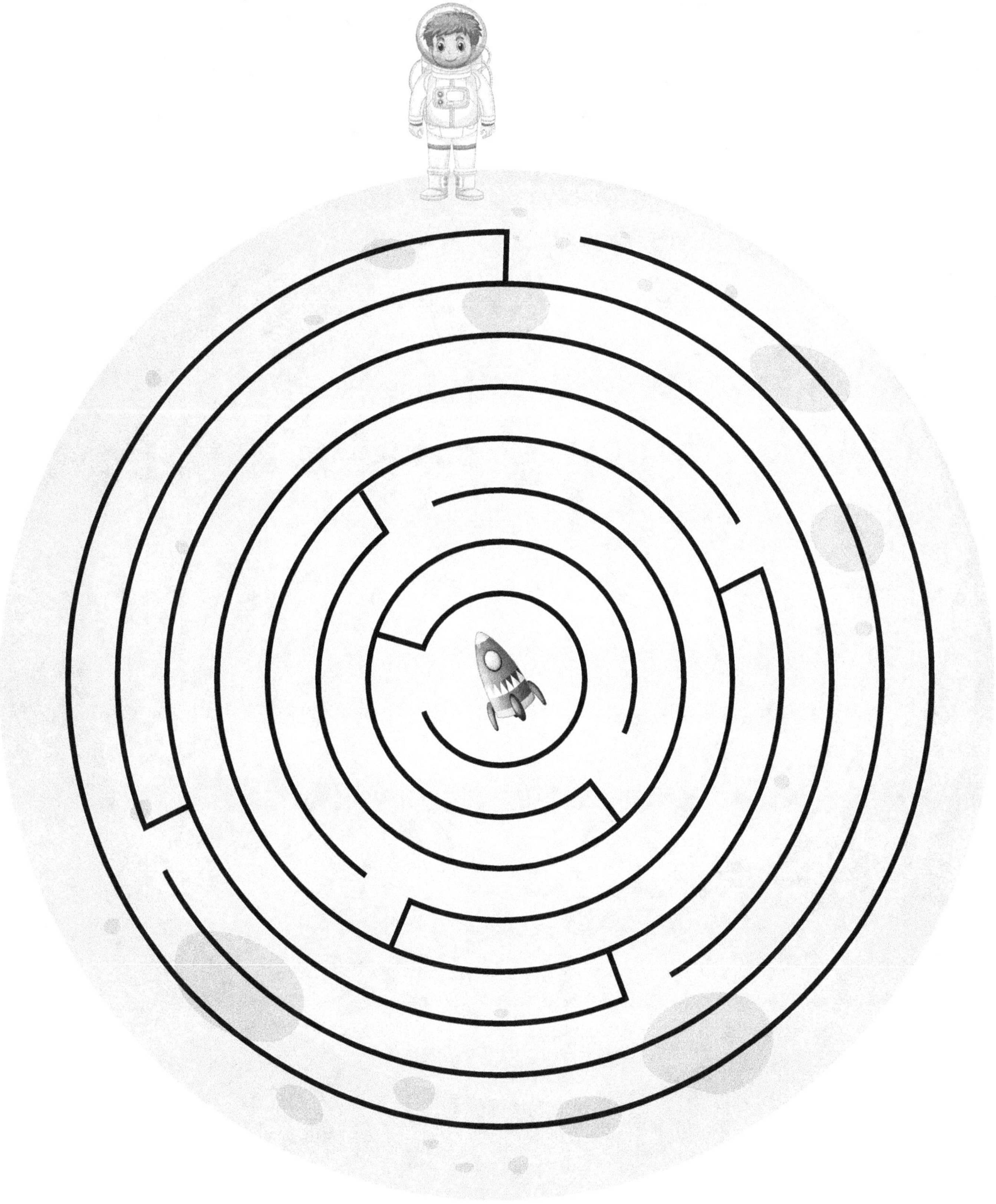

www.ingramcontent.com/pod-product-compliance
Lightning Source LLC
Chambersburg PA
CBHW081014170526
45158CB00010B/3037
* 9 7 8 1 0 9 8 7 5 6 0 9 3 *